D0388392

Greeting 101:

Easy Steps to Greeting
in the Local Church

by
Buddy Bell

Harrison House
Tulsa, Oklahoma

05 04 03 02 01   10 9 8 7 6

Greeting 101:
Easy Steps to Greeting in the Local Church
ISBN 1-57794-022-9
Copyright © 1998 by Buddy Bell
P. O. Box 27366
Tulsa, Oklahoma 74149

Published by Harrison House, Inc.
P. O. Box 35035
Tulsa, Oklahoma 74153

Greeting 101:

Easy Steps to Greeting in the Local Church

Contents

Acknowledgments

I want to thank my wife, Kathy, and my daughters Jennifer, Brandee, Stephanie and Kendra. They have always believed in and supported the calling and the anointing that was upon me and this ministry. Behind every man of God, there is a great woman of God.

I also want to thank Regina Mays for her devoted friendship and help in writing this book for greeters.

Dedication

I dedicate this book to all the faithful greeters throughout the world, to George Cormeir, a true servant of God, and to my two granddaughters: Mikaéle Davis and Shelby Harger.

You Are a V.I.P.

1
You Are a V.I.P.

Being a greeter, or a host and hostess as some churches call them, involves more than just standing at the door and shaking people's hands as they enter the church. It is a ministry. First Corinthians 12:28 calls it the ministry of helps. You are helping the pastors fulfill the vision God has given them by making those who come through the doors of the church feel at home. You help people feel joy. You help people feel love. You help people feel needed. You help people feel wanted. You help people feel sincerity. You help people feel important. You help people feel peace and comfort. You help people feel, most of all, welcomed.

Greet the Visitors

As a greeter in your church, it is your primary responsibility to let visitors know they are welcome. As a visitor, they are a guest of your church. When they pass through the church doors, it is your responsibility to see that they are served and that their needs and concerns are met. It is your responsibility to see that they are comfortable and treated hospitably.

"But how do you know if someone is a visitor?" That is what I asked the Holy Spirit one day. Do you know what He said? He said, "Visitors aren't hard to spot. Ninety-nine percent of them will step into the building, take six or seven steps, then stop to look around." So, when you see someone go through this routine, you can feel confident in walking over to them and saying, "I bet you're a visitor, aren't you?" Of course, they will say something like, "Well, how did you know?" Then you tell them, "Well, I've been doing this for years," and smile.

Then, you can take them by the arm and show them around the building. While you are walking with them down the hall, you can carry on a conversation with them about the church and tell them about what God is doing in the church. Tell them stories about how the church began. Such as how the pastor was in his bedroom when God woke him up in the middle of the night and told him, "I'm going to make you a pastor, and I'm going to send you to Springfield, Missouri. I'm going to raise up a great work there, and I'm going to send people from everywhere — north, south, east and west to become a part of the vision I have given to you."

As you walk along give them an opportunity to talk about themselves and their family. Listen carefully to all they say. If you ask them a question, make sure it isn't imposing. In doing this, you will help them feel valued.

Another way to locate visitors is to scan the back of the church just before the service begins. If you see a mother standing up with a baby in her arms, she is most probably a visitor. So, walk over to her, and let her know that you are a greeter at the church. Talk with her a little while to put her at ease then tell her about the nursery that is available and encourage her to take her child there. Hopefully, by then, she will feel comfortable enough to follow you to the nursery and leave her baby in the care of the nursery workers, so that she can enjoy the service.

At the end of the service, pay close attention, if they announce the visitors or have them stand up. If you see someone stand up who slipped through the door that you didn't know was a first time visitor, then make it a point to go up to that person after the service is over and tell them how good it was to have them here. Ask them if they have any questions then answer them as best as you can.

By doing this, you will make them feel at home, and they will want to come back the next week.

Greet All the Brethren

Once you are born-again, you are a member of the Body of Christ and you have your own particular function within that Body. As a greeter, you are the host or hostess, and you are in the church not only to make the visitors feel welcome but also to greet the leaders and brethren. (Heb. 13:24.)

As a greeter in the house of God, you can effectively serve God and receive blessings without limit. Now you may say to yourself, "But I thought that to *really* serve God and receive blessings without limit a person had to stand behind the pulpit." But in God's eyes, that simply isn't the case. You can effectively serve God by standing at the doors of your church and ministering to people as they come in, *and* you can receive blessings of no limit.

I'm reminded of an incident several years ago. We had a back door in the church that wasn't a popular spot with the greeters because very few people came through that door. But I had to make sure that I rotated everyone's assigned position. One Sunday, I asked my number one greeter to go to that door. At first, she hesitated, but then she corrected her attitude, and she accepted the position.

After the service, the greeter told me that as she stood by the door that morning just worshipping and praising God, an elderly lady walked through the door. My greeter hugged the woman and welcomed her to the church. She said the woman walked down the hall about twenty feet, stopped, turned around and came back. The woman then pulled a diamond ring off her finger, placed it in the greeter's hand and said,

"God just spoke to me and told me to give you this ring."

Now, I'm not saying that God will give you a diamond ring every time you stand and greet people by a door where you'd rather not have to stand. But I am saying that God will bless you spiritually and reward you in ways that are even more valuable than the beautiful diamond ring that particular greeter received when you are willing to serve Him in ways and in places that seem insignificant and unnoticed.

Greet the Anointed

Not only will you have an opportunity to minister to the visitors and the brethren, but you will have an opportunity to minister to your pastors, their wives, staff members, guest speakers and other anointed men and women of God. I don't know about you, but I have always found it a little humorous to watch the extent to which people will go in their attempt to be near the anointing of God.

They usually come early to the service so that they can sit up front. They are just hoping and praying that the man or woman of God will touch them or wave their arm in their direction because they know that it is the anointing that breaks the yoke. Sometimes though, I would think, "If you would just get involved in your church and be a greeter, all kinds of anointed men and women of God would walk through that door and touch you."

I usually tell my greeters to stand at the door and act like a vacuum so that when anointed men and women of God walk through the door, they can draw upon all of the anointing they want. When the speaker walks through the door, I tell them to kick it into double speed and draw all they can. Then when someone comes through the door who needs the anointing, they can pass the power of God on to them.

You don't have to get into a spat with your spouse about trying to arrive early so you can sit up front to be near the anointing. All you have to do is stand at the door and greet people as they come through in order to stay filled up. You can be as close to the anointing as you like.

Remember, as a greeter, you have been chosen to welcome all those who enter into His courts. You are a V.I.P., a very important person, in the Body of Christ.

Representatives of
the Kingdom of God

2

Representatives of the Kingdom of God

When visitors and church members walk through the door of the church, you are the first person they see. And, believe it or not, what people see first is what they believe they will continue to see. Even though the worship hasn't started yet, they have received, through you, a glimpse of what is to come.

You are an ambassador of the Most High God to His people, and you need to look and act your best because you are standing in His behalf. Colossians

3:17 TLB admonishes us saying, And whatever you do or say, let it be as a representative of the Lord Jesus.

In a very real way, you are also an extension of your pastor and his wife. You may be thinking to yourself, "If being a greeter is such an important position, then shouldn't the pastor and his wife be the ones to greet the people as they enter into the church?" But, as you and I know, the pastor and his wife can't be everywhere at once. If they had to greet everyone who walked through the door, the church service wouldn't start on time. Not only that the pastor wouldn't have the opportunity to still his mind and spirit before coming out to preach. So that is why they have asked you and me to assist them. Just by being a greeter, you help the pastors fulfill the vision that God has given to them.

Follow the Leader in Attire

As far as dress is concerned, I use this simple rule of thumb with my greeters: follow the examples of your pastor and his wife. If your pastor always seems to wear a suit and tie at the Sunday morning service, then the men should wear a suit and tie if they are greeting at the doors. If your pastor's wife is wearing a dress, then the ladies should wear dresses.

If on Wednesday nights, the pastor wears an open collar shirt, and he does this quite often, then I think it is okay for the men to wear open collar shirts. If the wife comes in a pantsuit outfit or slacks, then I think the women should feel free to wear pantsuits and slacks.

You may say, "But Brother Bell, our pastor's wife wears a new dress every week and gets her hair done all the time." Well, then you ought to have a new dress every week and get your hair done all the time, too! Now, all of you ladies might be saying, "Amen," about now and all of you men, "Oh, me." But seriously, whether or not you carry it to that extent, do remember that you are representing the pastor and his wife and, as a greeter, you should follow their example when it comes to your attire.

Cleanliness Is Next to Godliness

One time one of my greeters said, "Brother Bell, I want chapter and verse on why I have to wash my hands before I go to the door to greet people." I said, "Great! Turn to Second Corinthians 7:1. Notice that it says here, let us cleanse ourselves from all filthiness of the flesh. In other words, wash your hands!" Of course, I was just kidding with her, but there is some truth in what I'm saying here.

Now, some people don't need to be told to wash their hands, but some people do. Please understand that, most of the time, it isn't their fault, that is the way they were raised. I can talk about people like this because at one time in my life I was one of them.

I remember when I came to church for the first time. I was a farm boy from Illinois who had a high school education. I didn't have running water or an inside bathroom until I got married. I didn't own a suit, and I only took a bath once a week because I would always have to heat up two hot kettles and pour them into the old steel tub hanging out on the porch along with one cold kettle in order to bathe myself. It was quite a task.

As far as mouthwash was concerned, I didn't even know what it was. I remember the first time that I came to church and listened to someone go over the guidelines for being a greeter which included using mouthwash. I remember thinking to myself, "How do you wash your mouth?" It just didn't register with me.

Thank God, they didn't single me out. If they had singled me out and said, "Brother, you need to use a little mouthwash," my first response would have been, "What is mouthwash? And why are you telling *me* this?" I might have been hurt and left the church altogether.

It is usually easier to help a person in a group than it is to single them out. Eventually I figured out what mouthwash was, and I began to use it. It changed me and made a better person out of me. Now I use mouthwash all of the time and take a bath every day. I own more than one suit and tie and have discipline in my life.

I didn't have discipline in my life at that time. Now I'm so disciplined that one person asked me if I stack my change at night before I go to bed. Of course, my response was, "Doesn't everybody? Quarters go on quarters, dimes on dimes, nickels on nickels and pennies on pennies."

None of these changes came about in my life until I became involved in my church and was given some guidelines. Guidelines are important. I recognized that I needed to follow the guidelines as they were given if I wanted to serve where I believed God wanted me to serve. After I began to follow their guidelines, I noticed that more people held longer conversations with me. More people had more fellowship time because I was now using mouthwash and wearing underarm deodorant! I even got to the point that I would carry breath mints around with me or one of those little spray bottles.

Do an Attitude Check

Not only is your appearance important but so is your attitude. The person walking in the door thinks that your attitude is the attitude of the pastor and his wife. If you have a bad attitude when you greet someone, they may approach the sanctuary thinking, "If this is the attitude at the door, then this must be the attitude at the pulpit. And if this is the attitude of the minister who is ministering the Word of God, I'm going to have a hard time receiving from this church. So, maybe I'd better go somewhere else."

This poor soul hasn't even made it into the sanctuary yet, and already they are thinking about turning around and walking out the door after having met you. Your attitude and the spirit in which you receive people has a lot to do with how they will receive from the minister during the service. If you are in a bad mood and you pass that on to others as you are greeting, then they won't be able to receive what they need to receive.

So if you have cares and strife, leave them outside the church door when you come in and stir up the peace and joy of God within you instead so you can be a blessing to those you welcome. One church I visited had a unique idea to help remind them of this very thing.

They fixed up a trash can for the greeters and placed it just outside the church door. On the trash can was a little sign that said, "Place All Cares and Strife Here." So when the greeters arrived at church and saw that trash can, they were reminded to leave their cares and their strife outside.

Now I am not suggesting that every church get a trash can and put it outside of their church door, but I am suggesting that when you as greeters walk through those doors that you have some way of checking out your attitude. If you notice one of the other greeters seems to be a little down this week, then sincerely ask them how they are doing. Sometimes just the simple act of listening can help to lift another person's burden. Or you may want to address it more indirectly and just give that person a hug or a smile and let them know that they are loved regardless of what they may have faced that previous week. Maybe just a short prayer with that person will be all that is required to help them make the necessary adjustment in their attitude before going to the door.

Of course, the person you are totally responsible for is yourself. So make sure when you enter that church door that you have done whatever is necessary to have the kind of attitude that would be uplifting and encouraging to someone else. I am saying all of this not to be negative or harsh, but to impress upon you how vitally important you and your ministry are to the church and to those that God brings to the church. First impressions are critical, and your appearance and attitude can make the difference between someone being drawn closer to God or being pushed further away.

Getting Started

3
Getting Started

Now that you are appropriately dressed and have made whatever attitude adjustments are necessary, you are ready to begin greeting people. But before you do, there are a few more important things you need to know.

Arrive Early

All greeters should arrive at least thirty minutes before a service starts. As I have shared with greeters before, it is hard to minister to people who come in before you do. If you arrive twenty minutes after the main body of your church does, you have missed greeting most of the people. As a result, they are now seated in their seats with the same bad attitudes and problems they brought with them, and it will be harder for the pastor to minister to them.

If, on the other hand, you had arrived at the church before they did, you would have had the opportunity to deal with some of the burdens they were carrying. And it is more likely that they would have left those burdens outside the door.

I understand that every church is different. In some churches, people will arrive an hour before the service. In other churches, it will be fifteen to thirty minutes before the service. In some churches, the people don't show up until church starts or even after the service begins!

You need to figure out when the people in your church begin to arrive, then make sure that you arrive before they do. In other words, you want to be the first one at the doors. Of course, there will always be other workers who arrive early, but that isn't the concern. What matters is that the greeters arrive *before* those who are being seated in the church, the main body of believers.

If the greeters arrive when the people arrive, it will be too late, because there are some things you need to do before you take your position at the door. One of those things is to pray.

Always Begin With Prayer

As greeters, you need to come together and pray before you even go to your doors. Remember, however, that this isn't a prayer meeting. This is just a prayer before the service to prepare you for your particular ministry in the church. All you need to do is to ask God to assist you in being the best greeter you can be today.

You can pray for the pastor and the leaders in the church as well as for the people whom you will be greeting at the doors. You can pray for the service and for the work of God that will be accomplished in the service. But you don't have to pray for the whole church, the missionaries and the construction workers on the new building. All you need to do is to gather together, say your prayer, say amen, then go on and *do* what you were praying about.

What you want to avoid is a situation where the head greeter says, "Okay, everybody, let's gather around so we can pray before we go out." Then everybody gathers around, and just about the time that everybody has taken the hand of the person next to them, somebody starts in praying and praying and praying. After awhile, you think that they are never going to stop.

Eventually the music starts in the sanctuary, but they keep on praying. By now, numerous prayers are being prayed — prayers of deliverance and prayers that the person will stop praying soon! At this point, you are no longer in unity. You are in disunity. And instead of harmony, you are in discord. This, of course, isn't the kind of attitude you want your people to pass on to the people they will greet.

The best way to avoid a situation like this is to designate a person to start the prayer and another person to finish it. Make sure that everyone understands that all they need to pray about is their responsibilities and that the other ministries will pray for their responsibilities. Then you need to get to the doors and do what you have been praying about!

Two or More at Each Door

I think you need at least two people at each door, and if you are a larger church, you will need even more. As a matter of fact, if you have over two hundred people, I would say that you need six or seven people at each door.

Why is it necessary to have so many greeters at each door? If you have enough greeters, then some will be free to leave the door and assist people as necessary. I particularly like the idea of having a husband and wife team because they usually work well together. The husband can open the church door for people as they enter and be available to offer an umbrella when it is raining or a helping hand when someone needs assistance in getting out of the car. The wife can introduce mothers to the nursery workers and the children to the children's ministry workers so that they will be excited to be a part of what the other children are doing.

Whenever possible, I tell my greeters to encourage the children to be a part of the children's ministry rather than encouraging them to sit in the sanctuary. In the children's ministry, they will be able to learn about God and the Bible at their level. Of course, it also gives the mom and dad an opportunity to be in the sanctuary by themselves, free to worship and praise God without having to be concerned about Johnny or Susie standing on the seats or crawling under them.

As far as the nursery is concerned, be sure and take those couples with a baby to the nursery and explain to them that it isn't just a baby-sitting service but that it is a ministry. Tell them that the nursery workers are qualified to minister to and take care of their little one. Then be sure and give the new parents a copy of the guidelines that the workers in that ministry have to follow. Say, "We want you to have this, Mom. We want you to see the guidelines our workers have to follow so you will know what is going on in here." This will help to reassure them that their little one is in good hands and will be taken care of properly while they are in the service.

When you finish showing them around, escort them back to the door where they entered and turn them over to a friendly usher who will help them find a good seat. Then after the pastor preaches and the service is over, they will walk out saying, "Man, I feel as though I've been coming to this church for years!" Why? Because they know all about it. They don't have to come back six times before they work up enough nerve to ask somebody where the nursery is located. They were welcomed on their first visit. Most likely, they will be back.

Extending a
Warm Welcome

4
Extending a Warm Welcome

I believe that one of the most important aspects of our job as greeters is to surround every person who walks through the door of the church with the love of God. This can be done with a smile, handshake, kind word or a hug. How we communicate isn't as important as what we communicate, and what we communicate always needs to be positive, constructive and supportive.

A Warm Smile

A smile helps draw people to you. It expresses joy, cheer and happiness. It sends signals of welcome and friendliness and says without words a warm hello. Proverbs 15:30 TLB calls a smile a cheerful look and says that it brings joy to the heart just like good news gives health to the bones. A smile helps to create a loving, accepting atmosphere so that people can better receive the ministry that they so desperately need.

A Firm Handshake

A handshake is another way of greeting a person and letting them know that they are welcome. If you extend your hand, most people will respond by extending theirs as well. Avoid having your handshake be so spineless that the person feels as though they are shaking hands with a fish, and avoid having your handshake be so strong that the person is brought to their knees because of your vice grip. Make sure your handshake is neither weak nor too strong. See instead that it is firm. If it is firm, it will convey to the person in a positive way a little bit about who you are and what you believe.

A firm handshake is usually received well by both men and women, so don't hesitate to extend your hand when you see someone approaching the door. Of course, before you shake their hand, make sure that you have made eye contact with them. Then when you shake their hand, add to it a kind word or greeting.

A Kind Word

Watch your words and make sure that they are always kind. See that your greetings are never stiff, boring or self-oriented. A simple, "Good morning," "Hello," "Welcome" or "How are you?" are all greetings that can make a person feel welcomed and may even lead into a conversation. If a person you have greeted stops to talk or ask a question, be friendly and answer his or her question as best as you can.

While you are talking, remember: It isn't just what you communicate through your words and your gestures but also what you communicate through your spirit that makes an impact on a person. As a matter of fact, what you communicate with your spirit is so powerful that it will often override whatever you may be saying through your words or gestures. A greeter who is effective in word and spirit will be a major asset to any ministry.

Just a Simple Hug

Sometimes just a simple hug is all a person needs to feel welcomed and encouraged. A hug expresses gentleness, love and expectation. Hugs can go a long way in communicating love. They go a little further than a smile, handshake or kind word. As a matter of fact, hugs can actually minister healing through touch. They can help relieve pain and depression. Hugs can make the healthy happier and the most secure among us even more so. Hugs feel good and help us to overcome fears and ease tension. Hugs make happy days happier and impossible days possible.[1]

But the kind of hug you choose to use makes a difference because all hugs weren't created equal. Some hugs are for your honey only while others can be given to total strangers. All you have to do is pick the right hug for the right person on the right occasion.

The A-Frame Hug

The A-frame hug is most appropriate and comfortable for shy and unpracticed huggers, used to greet new friends

---

[1] Kathleen Keating, "A Hug for All Reasons," Photocopy, n.d., n.p.

and some acquaintances. In the A-frame hug, your arms go around each other's shoulders while you press your cheeks together, but not your bodies. This hug is non-threatening, usually brief, and is one way to say, "hello" or "good bye."[2]

The Cheek-to-Cheek Hug

The cheek-to-cheek hug is a tasteful way for two people who are seated or standing to greet each other or for one who is standing to greet the other person who is sitting. In this hug, you simply press the sides of your faces together so that you are cheek to cheek. This hug expresses deep feelings of kindness, a wordless "I'm sorry" or the sharing of a joyous and happy occasion. It can be used

[2] Keating, n.p.

to greet an elderly friend or close friends. This hug is considered to be very tender, gentle and even spiritual in nature.[3]

The Side-to-Side Hug

When a man hugs a lady, I believe that the side-to-side hug is the safest way to go. This kind of hug demonstrates a certain amount of respect towards the woman, and I also believe that their husbands appreciate it. A hug like this cuts down on the mixed messages that often occur when men and women hug.

The Heart-to-Heart Hug

The heart-to-heart hug would be most appropriate for greeting immediate family members, husbands and wives or

---

[3] Keating, n.p.

for friends who are like family with whom you have spent time. In other words, this hug is for people you feel close to and know well. It usually begins with direct eye contact between two people who are facing one another, then it ends up with both people wrapping their arms around each other and their bodies touching. This hug acknowledges the center place of each of us where pure, unconditional love is found. The heart-to-heart hug is heart-centered, lingering, caring and full of compassion.[4]

The Gradual Hug

Even though hugging is certainly a part of greeting, sometimes you will find

---

[4]   Keating, n.p.

that some people will come through your door who simply don't like being hugged. Maybe you will sense their resistance as they walk towards you at the door. Maybe the wife has already told you, "I'll bring my husband to church, but, remember, he doesn't like to be hugged." Or maybe someone has said to the head greeter, "Would you tell your people that my friend doesn't like to be hugged."

Now the question becomes, "How do you hug someone you know doesn't like being hugged?" The answer is that you do it gradually. You don't grab him and hug him the first week you see him because, if you do, he won't be back the next week.

All you do the first week is make eye contact with him and say, "Hi, brother, Jesus loves you," then you let him go on by. In other words, all you hope to accomplish in that first greeting is to get his attention and let him know that you have seen him and are aware of him.

The next time that he comes, make eye contact and reach out to shake his hand. If he responds, go ahead and shake his hand, then let him go on by. The next week when he comes shake his hand and say, "Praise the Lord, brother, God bless you."

The next week shake his hand with your right hand, then place your left hand on top of his hand while he his shaking your hand. Each week thereafter

gradually work your way up to his elbow
with your left hand. Then after about six
weeks, when you feel the time is right,
shake his hand and pull him towards you
to give him half of a heart-centered hug.
If he responds positively, then the next
week just put your arms all the way
around him in a man to man way, or, if it
is a woman, in a woman to woman way.
You will be surprised at the impact a hug
like this will make on a person, especially
one that isn't used to being hugged.

Now, you may be saying to yourself,
"Is it worth it to remember that this
person is a little uncomfortable about
being hugged?" If you want to see lives
changed and people helped, it is because
a hug can make all the difference in the

world. As a matter of fact, some articles that I have read claim that a hug can lift depression and even improve the body's immune system.[5] Researchers have also discovered that "when ill people are treated by the laying-on of hands, a significant change occurs in the hemoglobin component of their red blood cells."[6] One study showed that the immune system was directly affected in that the balance between the helper T-cells and the suppressors were altered in

---

[5] "Have You Hugged Your Kid Today?" Photocopy, n.d., n.p. Also see Tom Harpur, *The Uncommon Touch: An Investigation of Spiritual Healing*, (Plattsburgh: McClelland & Stewart Tundra Books, 1995), p. 143,144.

[6] Harpur, p. 138.

a positive way.[7] Now, I don't claim to be any research scientist, but I do happen to know the simple fact that there is power in a touch.

I remember one man who testified that he came to our church one morning with so much pain in his arm that he couldn't lift it above his head. He said that when he shook hands with the greeter at the door, he felt the power of God go into him. After he walked into the sanctuary and sat down, he realized that all pain was gone. He came back to the door rejoicing, telling us what God had done. We praised God with him as he went back in the sanctuary healed and worshipping the Lord with his hands

---

[7] Harpur, p. 145.

lifted high. No doubt he was able to receive far more from the ministry of the Word with his body free from pain than if he had to struggle with that kind of discomfort. God began ministering to that man at the door when he was healed by God's power released through a simple touch—a handshake.

Of course, Jesus also knew that there was power in a touch. Just look at how many people he touched. In Matthew 8:3, he reached out and touched the untouchable, a man with leprosy, and immediately he was cleansed. Later, in the same chapter, He touched the hand of Peter's mother-in-law, and the fever she had left her (v. 15). Then there is the time that two blind men came to Jesus crying for mercy, and He touched their eyes saying, According to your faith be it unto you. And they received their sight. (Matt. 9:27-30.)

Another man came to Jesus who was deaf and dumb. Jesus did something a little unusual to this man. He stuck his fingers in his ears then spit and touched his tongue! Can you imagine what that man may have been thinking at that moment? Yuck! Yet, it was in the next moment that the same man could hear and talk again. (Mark 7:33-37.) Then, of course, there was the time that a widow was burying her only son. She and her friends were carrying his coffin down the street to the graveyard, like they did in those days, and Jesus came by and touched the coffin. And do you know that the young man in that coffin sat up and began to speak? Jesus knew all about the power of touch, and He didn't hesitate to use it.

Sometimes we think that only the church believes in the laying-on of hands and the power of touch, but now even the medical profession is beginning to believe. As a matter of fact, they are taking bold steps to document the positive effect of touch using what they call Therapeutic Touch (TT). They have even founded a Touch Research Institute at the University of Miami's medical school to look into it! Already they have had some promising preliminary results in "promoting growth in premature babies, treating depression in teenage mothers, encouraging communication by autistic children, and boosting the immune system of people with AIDS."[8]

Now if touch can be proven to be this beneficial to the body, how much more beneficial must it be to the spirit? Maybe it would be through your touch that a person would actually be able to sense the presence of God or the love of God for the first time in their life. Think of what a difference that could make in their eternal destiny.

Is it worth the extra effort that it takes to hug someone? Well, let me ask you a question, "Is it worth it to have one more person come to know Jesus?" If

---

[8] Harpur, p. 143.

your answer is yes, then the extra effort is worth it. Remember, the healing process, whether spiritual or physical, begins with your handshake at the door.

Called to a Ministry of Love

5
Called to a Ministry of Love

As a greeter, you and I are called to a ministry of love, the God kind of agape love. When you receive a person at the door with an attitude of love, it can minister to both the giver and the receiver. Shaking a person's hand, giving them a smile and a kind word indicates welcome, but when you add to that the true love of God, it can develop into more. It can actually change a person's attitude, enabling them to receive the Word of God in a more powerful and effective way. God isn't limited in the

way that He expresses His love for us
and through us.

Expect a Miracle

Sometimes people come to church
with a burden so heavy that it is hard to
bear. But when the love of God touches
them, the burden they were carrying
absolutely falls to the floor. I remember
one time when a greeter grabbed
somebody's hand and shook it, and the
person just broke out into tears and
began to weep crying, "Oh, my God, I
need Jesus."

Now, keep in mind that this
happened at the doors of the church
before anyone had even come into the
service. Sometimes we have the false

idea that the only time and place a person can get saved is in the sanctuary at the end of a service during an altar call. But we have to realize that Jesus is everywhere. He doesn't just show up at the end of the sermon. Why should a person have to sit all the way through a sermon and hear the Word of God from an unsaved person's perspective when they could be saved at the doors and hear the Word of God as a child of God?

The only reason this hasn't happened more often is because we haven't been expecting it. Sometimes we only think of people receiving their sight or having their hearing restored as being a miracle, but when someone receives Jesus as their Lord and Savior, it is the greatest miracle of all. And we can rejoice when God chooses to use us to bring His salvation to another person.

And just as He can use us to minister salvation, He can use us to minister healing. Do you remember the account of Philip in the book of Acts? He wasn't an apostle. He was just a believer like you and me. But do you remember what happened when he went down to the city of Samaria in Acts 8:5-8? The lame walked and the unclean spirits came out, and there was great joy in that city. If God can use Philip, He can use someone like you and me if we will only dare to believe.

Come Prepared To Minister

The importance of greeters being filled to overflowing with the love of God cannot be stressed enough. As a matter of fact, First Corinthians 13:4-8 TLB should be the daily confession of all greeters:

> I am very patient and kind, never jealous or envious, never boastful or proud, never haughty or selfish or rude. I do not demand my own way. I am not irritable or touchy. I do not hold grudges and will hardly even notice when others do me wrong. I am never glad about injustice, but rejoice whenever truth wins out. If I love someone I will be loyal to him no matter what the cost. I will always believe in him, always expect the

best of him, and always stand my ground in defending him.

We must always remember that our battle isn't against flesh and blood, but it is against principalities and powers in high places. And one of our greatest weapons is love.

Now I'm the type of person who believes in having fun in church and in experiencing the joy of the Lord. But I'm also very serious when it comes to church because I realize that people who come to the services have overwhelming concerns. Others are contemplating suicide. Some are contemplating divorce. Some are contemplating using drugs or becoming a member of a gang because of peer pressure.

We don't know what a particular person may be facing when they walk through the door of the church. That is why we need to be very sensitive to the needs of each person and be prepared to minister to them.

Reaching the Hard Cases

Standing at the door and greeting people was the first ministry I oversaw in my church. I was the head greeter, and I loved standing at the door to welcome people into the church. But I didn't just look for people that had a smile on their face. I looked for the hard cases.

Sometimes I would even listen for slamming doors out in the parking lot. When I heard a door slam, I knew I had a challenge on my hands. Eventually I'd see them heading towards the church door from the parking lot. I would wait for them to reach the door. Why? Because I was going to drive out that attitude. I was going to smother that person with the love of God. I was going to let them know that they were important and that God loved them and that I wanted them to receive everything that God had for them.

But with their attitude, I knew they were going to have a hard time. So, it became my ministry to give that person something that could replace their attitude: the love of God.

Eventually our church was known for its love. People would say, "Man, there is so much love in this church. Why?" And I believe with all my heart it was because love was the first thing we gave away before our service started. You receive from people what you give. Luke 6:38 TLB puts this truth into words when it says, Whatever measure you use to give — large or small — will be used to measure what is given back to you.

So when a person is met with the love of God as soon as they enter the church, they want to give that love to somebody else who in turn wants to give it to somebody else. When that happens, before you know it, you'll look up, and everybody is sharing the love of God.

Walking, Talking Information Centers

6

Walking, Talking Information Centers

As a greeter, you not only extend a warm welcome to those coming through the doors and surround them with the love of God, you also help keep the vision of the church alive. You are the walking, talking information centers of the church, and you should know everything there is to know about your church.

If people have any questions about the church, they will usually figure that someone with a name tag on knows about the church, and they will come to you, the greeter, for answers. That is why you should always wear your name tag before, during and after every service. And should also be aware of what is going on in the church.

Answering Questions

For example, you may be asked "How did the church get started?" "How many people have been saved since the church began?" "What miracles have you seen since you have been here?" "What is the pastor's vision?" "Do you have a children's ministry?" "Where is the nursery?" "What time does the evening service begin?"

Remember: no question is a dumb question and people ask certain questions for a reason. Always be considerate when you answer. And if you don't know the answer, ask one of the other greeters or see if the head greeter can come and answer the question. As much as possible, you want to be the one who can tell them about the church. But in order to be able to do that you will have to be informed about the church.

Attending Monthly Meetings

Where do you find all of this information? That is where your head greeter comes in. He/she should hold monthly meetings in which information about the history of the church and the events taking place will be discussed. Some head greeters may even put together a handout every month with

this kind of information on it as well.
The monthly meeting is a good place to
receive the answers to some of your
questions and to learn ways to do what
you have been called to do in an even
better way.

Announcements! Announcements! Announcements!

Some churches also give the greeters
a bulletin or announcements to hand to
people as they come through the doors.
This information usually helps to inform
everyone on the church's vision and
mission, activities and upcoming events,
service times and office hours as well as
tell them about the various ministry
departments of the church. So always
read over the bulletin or announcements

and refer to them when people ask questions about upcoming events.

Sometimes, within the pages of the bulletin, an offering envelope is also included. This can be used by the person to place their offering in when it is collected during the service. Some churches send a box of envelopes directly to the members homes on an annual basis while other churches have the ushers pass them out as needed in the service.

Personally, I recommend to our greeters that we not liberally hand out bulletins and offering envelopes to every child that comes through the door. "But they need something to scribble on," you may say. Well, why don't you make up a children's bulletin with pictures that they can color and word games they can figure out. Then give the children this bulletin instead? They will love it because it was made with them in mind. Also, you will save on the cost of bulletins and offering envelopes and be better stewards of the church's money.

Another way to keep people aware of upcoming events in the church is to post TV monitors with information about special dates and activities. Skits, church newspapers, bulletin boards and an information booth are also effective.

A Word on Faithfulness

Some churches ask that the greeters close the doors once the service begins and others wait until later. Find out from your head greeter exactly what the pastor wants you to do at your church.

Return any leftover bulletins or announcements to the head greeter or leave them in a place that he/she has designated. After this, you are free to go ahead and take your seat. If during the service, your church has the visitors stand up or has a place for them to go after the service for refreshments to meet the pastor, then be sure to make them feel welcome once again.

Of course, before you leave the service, make sure you have signed up for the next service when you will be a greeter. This is important because it lets the head greeter know who can be

counted on to be there at the next service.
Some head greeters have everyone sign
the sign-up sheet directly after the prayer
time before going to the doors. In either
case, make sure that the head greeter
knows when you will be back and that
you can be counted on to be dependable
and faithful.

Don't ever underestimate the importance of faithfulness. It doesn't matter
how big or how small the task is that
you have been given to do in the church.
The most important thing is that you
are faithful in whatever you put your
hand to do. First Corinthians 4:2 says,
Moreover it is required in stewards,
that a man be found faithful.

Requirements for Greeters

7
Requirements for Greeters

If as you have been reading, you feel that you may be called into the ministry of helps as a greeter and would like to look into it a little further, get in touch with the head greater at your church and see what requirements your church has to become a greeter. Each church, of course, will be a little bit different in what they require.

When I was the head greeter, I interviewed each greeter before placing them in the ministry. The following will give you an idea of what I did and what you might expect to find at your church.

Attend a Membership Class

First of all, I required that all hosts and hostesses complete or be in the process of completing a membership class, or foundations class as some churches call it. The reason for this is that everyone who greets needs not only to have made a commitment to Christ, but also they need to have made a commitment to the body of believers in the Church where they will be serving.

Such a course helps to clarify what the church believes. When everyone finishes the course, they are speaking the same thing, and there is no confusion. First Corinthians 1:10 puts it this way saying, Now I beseech you, brethren, by the name of our Lord Jesus Christ, that ye all speak the same thing . . . perfectly joined together in the same mind and in the same judgment.

If upon finishing the course, the person decides they are in agreement with what that particular church believes, then everyone will operate with the same vision and will speak the same thing. If, however, a person is unable to put their heart and soul into what the church believes, then there will be division, and people will begin to go in different directions. Eventually, discord will spring up. But, if everyone is in one accord, then they will have the same vision, and there will be unity.

Complete an Application

I also required that all greeters complete an application form when they came in for their interview with the head greeter. The application form was simply a way of getting some basic information about the greeters, such as their address and their phone number so I could contact them if need be. It also gave me an idea of their commitment to Christ and the areas of the church where they felt called to serve. The application form was usually pretty straightforward and not too lengthy.

Get an Interview

Once their application form was filled out, then I would sit down with the applicant for an interview. The purpose of the interview was to get to know the person applying and to give him/her an opportunity to ask any questions that he/she may have. The interview should be relaxed and informal, and everyone should just be themselves. Before making the final selection, however, I would always seek God's guidance in prayer.

Sign a Commitment Sheet

If after the interview, a decision was made to extend the opportunity to greet and the applicant accepted, then a commitment sheet was completed. Most people understand the need for an application to be filled out, but some haven't yet heard of a commitment sheet. In short, the commitment sheet simply expressed in writing the agreement that was being made between the greeter and me.

From what I have experienced, I believe a commitment sheet is a good idea. It clarifies exactly what the person is making a commitment to do and for how long. I usually leave a space at the bottom of the sheet so that greeters can sign their name and verify that they can be counted on to fulfill their commitment. Having them sign their name is important because there is just something about signing your name that helps you keep a commitment.

Be Committed

After greeters have made a commitment, it is important that they prove themselves faithful. If they can be depended upon in small things, then God will be able to trust them in greater things. Luke 16:10 puts it this way: He that is faithful in that which is least is faithful also in much.

Sometimes people become discouraged because what they are doing is not noticed by other people. But that really shouldn't matter because promotion doesn't come from man anyway. Promotion comes from God. So if you as a greeter have made a commitment to be at the doors to greet at a certain time, then be there because God and people are counting on you.

Some people have the tendency to over-commit themselves to activities.

Then when it's time to keep their commitment to greet at the church, they say that they need to stay home and spend some time with their family.

At first, when I heard this excuse, it sounded reasonable, so I would just let it go on by. But I don't buy that as an excuse anymore because there is plenty of time in a week to do all that is needed for your family *and* to keep your commitment at the church as a greeter.

One time I actually sat down and figured out how many hours we all had in a week. I was surprised by what I found. There are a total of 168 hours in a week. Forty hours of that are spent working. If you figure that a person sleeps eight hours a night, then fifty-six more hours are gone. And if they come to church three services a week for two hours each service, then six more hours are gone, and they are left with sixty-six hours to be with their family.

So when someone tells me that they now want to take part of the six hours set aside for church to be with their family, I have to question what it is that they are doing with the rest of those sixty-six hours. In most instances, it isn't a matter of time as much as it is a matter of priorities.

When you really think about it, there is plenty of time for most people to be with their family and to keep their commitment to be a greeter. If a person's priorities are in line, they can find time to serve in the church *and* to minister to the needs of their family. So once a person has made a commitment to be a greeter, they need to see it through.

Personally, I always recommend a training or probationary period of at least four weeks in order to see if the new greeters are serious about their commitment. During this time, I would give them a temporary name tag. Then, if after four weeks, they have proven themselves faithful and decide to continue, I would purchase a more permanent name tag for them.

From experience, I would say that this probationary training period is a good idea. It gives the new greeters an opportunity to see if this is really what they expected and if they want to commit themselves to it in the coming year. A waiting period also saves on the budget because you don't end up spending two or three dollars for a name tag that is only used once or twice. Establishing a training or probationary period is simply good stewardship.

Finish the Process

The interviewing process is helpful to both the person signing up to be a greeter and the person looking for greeters. It gives the greeter an opportunity to ask a few questions, and it allows the head greeter an opportunity to get an idea of whom he/she can rely on to be there when the doors to the church are opened.

Even though I realize that every church may not use this approach, I recommend it highly and have found it to work quite well.

The Qualifications
for Overseers

8
The Qualifications for Overseers

Acts 6:3, talks about the kind of person who should be an overseer of the ministry of helps in the church. It was written at a time when the widows weren't receiving care, the tables weren't being served and the people's needs weren't being met because the apostles were trying to do it all. Finally, they decided to attend to the Word of God and to appoint other people to oversee the other various tasks that needed to be done. So they laid out some specific qualifications that they were looking for and decided to choose some people to meet those needs.

Have an Honest Report

First of all, it says that they had to have an honest report. The only way you can have an honest report about yourself is through faithfulness. In other words, the only way another person can give an honest report about you is after having been around you. And if you haven't been around on a consistent basis, no one can really give an honest report about you.

If somebody came up to me and said, "Buddy, could you tell me something about the greeter who sometimes stands at the side door?" Well, if I was real honest, I'd have to say,

"I really couldn't give you an honest report because he hasn't been here that often. I could tell you what I have observed about him, but he hasn't been here often enough for me to know him."

So if you are a greeter who wants to be an overseer, you need to be faithful as a greeter first so that someone can give an honest report about you.

Be Full of the Holy Ghost

Second of all, it says they should be full of the Holy Ghost. When you are full of the Holy Ghost, then the love of God is clearly seen in your life. Of course, the best way to stir up the love of God on the inside of you is by praying in the Holy Ghost because Romans 5:5

says that the love of God is shed abroad in your heart by the Holy Ghost.

When you do, you will be amazed to see what a difference it will make in your interactions with people. As a matter of fact, many of the problems that you could have faced at the door or with your greeters can be taken care of in advance because you spent time in your prayer closet getting full of the Holy Ghost. When He fills you to that degree, all you have to do is look at a person, and the love of God flowing out from you will be able to set them free!

Be Full of Wisdom

Thirdly, it says that they should be full of wisdom. Wisdom is important for overseers because they will encounter various situations and people that will require God's wisdom in order to deal appropriately with the situation or person. For example, a church where I served was known as a family church. But I had mainly women working as greeters at the door. So I asked the women who were married to invite their husbands to stand with them at the doors. Having a couple stand together at the door was just another way of demonstrating that our church placed an emphasis on ministering to families.

I remember one man whose personality type would be described as an introvert. He was very withdrawn and rarely reached out to initiate conversations with others. But a short time after he began helping his wife greet visitors, he developed into one of our best greeters. He eventually became the head greeter.

If they have been a member for awhile and involved in several areas, they will also have a better working knowledge of the mission and ministry of the church and how it functions.

Be Full of Faith

Another quality that an overseer should have is to be full of faith. Stephen was one of the men chosen to be an overseer in the ministry of helps because he had all the qualities that they were looking for and was full of faith. (Acts 6:5.) Of course, we all know how faith comes — by the hearing of God's Word! (Rom. 10:17.)

So in order to be an overseer, the person should be a member of the church who attends services regularly. And not only should they know the Word of God, but they should be applying it in their life as well.

Set Apart for Service

I also believe that there should be a time set aside for those who are chosen to be overseers to be set apart for service. The pastor(s) should have prayer, then lay their hands on those called to oversee the ministry of helps just like the apostles laid hands on Stephen and the other men. (Acts 6:6.)

Ideally, the message of the sermon should be on serving so that the congregation will have a better understanding of how God esteems and rewards the one who will take on a servant's heart, like Jesus. Then, the greeters should be introduced to the congregation. Giving special attention in this way will accomplish several important needs: 1) presenting an area where other members of the congregation may feel called to serve, 2) encouraging the people to rightly esteem the value of the ministry of helps, and 3) making the greeter feel special and not taken for granted.

When men were set aside to follow through in the ministry of helps, Acts 6:7 goes on to tell of the tremendous increase in the work of God. I believe that it isn't any different today. Those who are called to be pastors in the church should be given the opportunity to give themselves to the study of God's Word and prayer, while those who are called to the ministry of helps need to assist and do whatever else is required to see that the vision of the church is fulfilled.

Tips for Overseers

9
Tips for Overseers

I am a motivator. I love to motivate and inspire people. Every department head or overseer should always seek to be a good motivator. Of course, part of being a good motivator is setting a good example.

Set the Example

As the overseer, you should be the first of the greeters to arrive. You should see that the doors are open for them. You should have a smile on your face and the love of God in your heart ready to embrace them when they arrive.

After you have led them in prayer and given them their bulletins or announcements to hand out, make sure that you have two or more greeters stationed at each door. Also be sure that you are free to move from door to door, to insure that everything is progressing smoothly. You are the overseer. That is what you are to be doing: Overseeing.

When I was overseeing my staff of greeters, I constantly moved from door to door, making sure they had what they needed to do their job well. If they ran out of bulletins, I brought them some more. If they had a question, I tried to answer it.

All the while, I was making sure that my greeters were stirred up in the love of God and were letting it flow out into the people they were greeting. If, for example I noticed that there was one greeter who wasn't greeting people like he should — perhaps he or she was carrying around a few cares — when their door wasn't too busy, I would go over and say, "What's wrong with you? Do you have a problem?" No, seriously, that is what I would not do!

Instead I would get right beside them and begin to greet people with them, or I might just walk up to them, shake their hand then pull them close to me and give them a big hug.

In other words, I would set an example for them to follow. I wouldn't tell them, "Hey, you need to be doing this or that." No, they are adults. They have a brain. They have the Holy Spirit at work inside of them. If shown what to do in the right spirit, eventually they would pick it up and start thinking, "That's the way I need to be shaking people's hands and hugging them." All I had to do was surround them with the love of God in order to motivate them in the right direction.

Have Regular Meetings

Then I always made sure that I had a meeting just for the greeters on a regular basis. Once a month seemed to work out well for me. If I ever had to change a meeting for some reason, I usually tried to make sure that I never let six weeks go by without having another meeting.

During these meetings, I would give them handouts with information about the church, answer questions and address specific needs. It was also a time for us to pray together for the church and its various ministries, as well as for the unsaved.

Regardless of how interesting the meeting was, I always tried to make sure that we started on time and ended on time. No meeting ever went much longer than forty-five minutes and everyone always knew just about what to expect when it came to a time commitment.

Of course, each group is different, and I wouldn't want to say that everyone has to do everything just like I did. Get started and then see what works. But whatever you do, don't underestimate the importance of conducting regular meetings because during these meetings different ideas are shared which the greeters can use to continue to improve themselves.

Prepare Handouts

One idea that proved to be quite successful was putting together a handout for every meeting. Usually I would include on these handouts some information about the history of the church, the vision of the pastor, the first and last names of all the staff members and their functions as well as a list of the various ministries currently going on in the church and who headed them up. When the greeters received this information, they could look them over and ask questions, which often provided a starting place for useful discussion.

These handouts helped inform my greeters about what was going on in the church as well as update them on what had already happened.

Give Quizzes

Then every three months, I would give them a quiz over the information that I had put on the handouts and what we had discussed in our meetings. The point of these quizzes wasn't to flunk people out and prevent them from being greeters. It was to challenge them to learn more about the church and to stir up their curiosity about various activities going on in the church. It also kept them accountable and helped motivate them to attend the meetings since they knew what had been discussed might show up on the quiz later. It also helped give them a feeling of accomplishment, because if they simply listened during the meetings they would usually do well on the quizzes.

Lead Discussions

After the quiz was over, we might have a more informal discussion about topics that the group raised. For example, we might talk about the pastor's vision and what stage of the vision we were in at the time. Or we might talk about new upcoming events that everyone should know. Sometimes I might just chose one of the following questions and discuss it:

1. What do we want our guests and visitors to feel?

2. What is our primary responsibility?

3. What will make visitors come back?

4. What are we trying to achieve?

5. How can we show people we care?

6. How can we express genuine interest in them?

7. How do we display a warm, favorable and friendly attitude?

8. How do we greet visitors?

9. What is the image of the church we are displaying?

These are just a few of the questions I used to ask, but whatever works for your particular group is what you will want to do.

Other important topics to cover with your group are hugging techniques, spiritual authority, and the need to have one or two scriptures to share with everyone.

It isn't something we like talking about, but in today's society it's important to be on guard — even in the church. Some churches in neighborhoods with noted violence even use metal detectors at the doorway to be certain people aren't carrying in a weapon of some kind. In a recent workshop, I told the greeters, "There are two reasons why you hug people. Number one, you hug them to give them the love of God. And number two, you hug them to make sure they aren't carrying anything!" Obviously, all churches aren't that way, but we are hearing more incidents of that nature.

It is important, too, for greeters to understand their spiritual authority in the name of Jesus Christ. (Matt. 28:18-20; Mk. 16:15-18; Eph. 2:4-6, 6:10-17.)

When a greeter is prayed up and tuned in to the spirit realm, he or she will be sensitive and alert to someone who may come to the service under the influence of an evil spirit with the intention of being disruptive or violent or under a spirit of oppression or depression. A greeter can take authority over the demonic spirit so that no disruption occurs and, if a person is bound, he or she can be loosed to receive from the Word and the presence of God in the service. Knowing your spiritual authority can help you to be sensitive to minister the love of God to people as they walk through the door.

A Prayer for Greeters

In closing, I would like to suggest that you, as an overseer and as a greeter, spend some time with God in prayer, seeking His face for guidance and direction. There is no substitute for spending time in His presence. He is the only One Who can really give you the kind of insight you need to be the overseer or greeter that He has called you to be. Come to Him with all of your concerns, and He will show you a way to make it through.

The following is an example of a simple prayer that you can adapt to your particular situation during your time alone with Him or during your time together.

Father, we thank You for giving us further insight into the ministry of helps which you have called us to fulfill. We realize that we are more than just people standing at the door shaking people's hands as they walk through, and that we play a vital part in seeing the vision You have given our pastor, come to pass.

We place ourselves in line with his vision, and desire to see those who don't yet know You be saved; those who need Your healing touch be made well; those who need deliverance be set free and those who have broken hearts be made whole.

As representatives of Your love, we will continue to remember to give out Your love to each person we come in contact with, knowing that we will never run out because it will be given back to us, pressed down, shaken together and running over.

We want to be better greeters in our churches. Thank You for speaking to our hearts so we can make the necessary changes needed, and for helping us to allow You to flow through us to the people that we touch. Fill us with Your Holy Spirit so we can surround everyone who comes through our doors with Your love and follow more closely in Your footsteps.

For all of this, we thank You in Jesus' name. Amen.

About the Author

Rev. Buddy Bell, president and founder of the Ministry of Helps International, Inc., in Tulsa, Oklahoma, originally began serving in the Ministry of Helps at his  local church by doing all his hands could find to do with excellence.

Sensitive to the leading of the Holy Spirit, Rev. Bell began developing highly effective methods of ushering, conspicuous only in their reflection of God's character and love. Ushers following his example or trained by him functioned supernaturally. As they maintained the order necessary to allow the power of the Holy Spirit to flow forth to minister, they spread God's love. People's needs were met not only in the services, but elsewhere in the church building—even in the parking lot. Consequently, churches began requesting Rev. Bell's usher and general Ministry of Helps training.

Rev. Bell began holding workshops, speaking at conferences, serving as a consultant to churches, filming videos and writing manuals and books to meet the need. His training, coupled with his hilarious presentation, have been in great demand. He has now traveled to more than 1,000 churches, teaching and helping church staffs and congregations awake to the power and plan of the Holy Spirit for accomplishing the work of the ministry through every believer.

Rev. Bell has authored *The Ministry of Helps Handbook*, revealing how to be totally effective serving in the ministry of helps. He has also produced "The

Complete Local Church Usher Training System," "Development of Local Church Leadership Notebook," "Development of Local Church Membership" and 20 videos utilized by more than 9,000 churches worldwide.

Rev. Bell's humor, zeal and anointing from God to present Ministry of Helps training motivates people in a most delightful manner to find their place and fulfill their ministry in the local church.

To contact Buddy Bell,
write:

Buddy Bell
P. O. Box 27366
Tulsa, Oklahoma 74149

E-Mail:
bb@mohi.org

Internet Website:
www.mohi.org

*Please include your prayer requests
and comments when you write.*

Other Products by Rev. Buddy Bell

Videos (VHS Only)

The Local Church Leadership Series

Faithfulness — the Crowbar of God

God Uses Both Stars and Candles

Jesus and the Ministry of Helps

Fear Not: Leadership, Organization
and Structure

Guidelines: Yes or No?

How To Motivate Volunteers

Straight Talk to Leadership

The Local Church Motivational Series

The Zeal of God

The Word Works

How To Close the Door on Strife and
Jealousy in the Local Church

Staying on Track With God

How To Deal With Burnout

Journey of a Servant

The Local Church Helps Series

> Understanding the Ministry of Helps
>
> Finding Your Place in the Local Church
>
> How to Relate to Your Pastor
>
> Winning First Time Visitors

The Local Church Servant Series

> Ushering, in the Local Church
>
> The First Look — Host and Hostess
>
> Why Minister to Children?

Computer Sites

Internet Website (www.mohi.org)

> All of our materials
>
> 15 seconds of video of each of our teachings

E-Mail (bb@mohi.org)

Manuals

The Complete Local Church Usher
Training System

> — the most complete course for
>   ushers available

— 2-hour video and 70-page
training manual

Development of Local Church Leadership
— bring organization and efficiency to
your local church
— 8 audio cassette lessons and study
notes on leadership

Development of Local Church Membership
— Everything you will need to make
ministers out of your members
— 4 video messages, workbook, spiritual
gift test, and more

Books

Ushering 101
The Ministry of Helps Handbook: How to
Be Totally Effective Serving in the Ministry
of Helps

Foreign Language Videos & Cassettes

Journey of a Servant

Fear Not: Leadership, Organization, &
    Structure Part 1 & 2

God Uses Both Stars and Candles

Becoming a Servant of Fire

Available Languages:

    Arabic, Chinese, German, Indonesian,
    Russian, Vietnamese, Spanish, Portuguese,
    Tagalog, Korean, Ukrainian, and Romanian

Available Formats:

    NTSC, PAL, SECAM, M-PAL, N-PAL, MESECAM

Additional copies of this book
available from your local bookstore.

HARRISON HOUSE
Tulsa, Oklahoma 74153

The Harrison House Vision

Proclaiming the truth and the power
Of the Gospel of Jesus Christ
With excellence;

Challenging Christians to
Live victoriously,
Grow spiritually,
Know God intimately.